TIMELINE

The Arab–Israeli Conflict

Cath Senker

W

FRANKLIN WATTS
LONDON•SYDNEY

First published in 2007 by Franklin Watts

Copyright © 2007 Arcturus Publishing Limited

Franklin Watts
338 Euston Road
London NW1 3BH

Franklin Watts Australia
Level 17/207 Kent Street, Sydney, NSW 2000

Produced by Arcturus Publishing Limited,
26/27 Bickels Yard, 151–153 Bermondsey Street, London SE1 3HA

The right of Cath Senker to be identified as the author of this work has been
asserted by her in accordance with the Copyright, Designs and Patents Act 1988.

Series concept: Alex Woolf
Project manager and editor: Helen Maxey
Designer: Simon Borrough
Picture researcher: Helen Maxey
Consultant: James Vaughan
Cartography: Location Map Services, Encompass Graphics

Picture credits:
Corbis: cover (Reuters/Corbis), 4, 5, 6 (Bettmann/Corbis), (Bettmann/Corbis), 7
(Hulton-Deutsch Collection/Corbis), 8, 10 (Bettmann/Corbis), 11 (Hulton-
Deutsch Collection/Corbis), 12, 13 (Bettmann/Corbis), 14 (Hulton-Deutsch
Collection/Corbis), 15, 16, 18 (Bettmann/Corbis), 19 (Owen Franken/Corbis), 20
(Bettman/Corbis), 21 (David Rubinger/Corbis), 22 (Bettmann/Corbis), 23
(Hulton-Deutsch Collection/Corbis), 24 (Simonpietri Christian/Corbis Sygma), 25
(Alain DeJean/Sygma/Corbis), 26 (Bettman/Corbis), 27 (David Rubinger/Corbis),
28 (Bettman/Corbis), 29 (Patrick Chauvel/Sygma/Corbis), 30 (Patrick
Robert/Sygma/Corbis), 31 (Peter Turnley/Corbis), 32 (Reuters/Corbis), 33
(Attar/Corbis Sygma), 34 (Pablo/Corbis Sygma), 35 (Koren Ziv/Corbis Sygma), 36
(Ricki Rosen/Corbis Saba), 37 (Corbis Sygma), 38, 39, 40 (Reuters/Corbis), 41 (Ed
Kashi/Corbis), 42 (Ronen Zvulun/Reuters/Corbis), 43 (Andrew Mills/Star
Ledger/Corbis), 44 (Doron Golan/Jini/Epa/Corbis), 45 (Lynsey Addario/Corbis).

Every attempt has been made to clear copyright. Should there be any inadvertent
omission, please apply to the publisher for rectification.

A CIP catalogue record for this book is available from the British Library.

Dewey Decimal Classification Number: 956.04

ISBN 978 0 7496 7187 7

Printed in China

Franklin Watts is a division of Hachette Children's Books.

Contents

First Zionist Congress

29 AUGUST 1897

On 29 August 1897, Austrian-Jewish journalist Theodor Herzl organized the First Zionist Congress. He wanted to win support from Jewish people worldwide for his idea to create a homeland where Jews could be safe from persecution. Held in Basel, Switzerland, the congress attracted about 200 delegates, mostly from central and eastern Europe and Russia. There were Jewish people from all walks of life – from the strictly religious to non-practising Jews, from students to businessmen.

ANTI-SEMITISM IN EASTERN EUROPE

In the 1880s, about 90 per cent of the world's Jews lived in Europe and Russia. At this time, there was growing anti-Semitism – hatred of the Jews – especially in Austria, Germany and France. In Russia, the government of Tsar Alexander III was becoming increasingly unpopular. The tsar blamed the problems of society on the Jews. He passed laws against them, for example, imposing new restrictions on where Jews could live and limiting the number who could go to university or work in the professions. Anti-Jewish feelings grew, and ordinary people launched pogroms – violent attacks on Jewish communities.

Some Jews did not react and hoped that the problems would pass. Others gave up their religious practices to try to fit in to Christian society. Many joined other Russians in protests against the tsar. Between 1891 and 1914, around 2.5 million Jews escaped from eastern Europe and Russia, mostly for the USA. A small minority, led by Theodor Herzl, came to believe that the only solution was for Jewish people to live separately from non-Jews.

INTERNATIONAL ZIONISM

At the First Zionist Congress, the Zionist Organization was established, with Herzl as president. Various places were considered as the site for the creation of a Jewish homeland. In 1904 the seventh Zionist Congress finally decided on Palestine.

This undated photo shows Theodor Herzl, who is seen as the founder of the Zionist movement.

TIMELINE	**THE BEGINNING OF ZIONISM 1881–1914**
1881–1882 ▶	Pogroms in Russia and Romania lead to mass emigration of Jews.
1881–1903 ▶	First aliyah – wave of Jewish immigration to Palestine.
1890–1913 ▶	The Ottoman rulers restrict Jewish immigration to Palestine.
1896 ▶	Herzl publishes a book called *The Jewish State*, in which he argues that the Jewish people need their own country.
29 August 1897 ▶	First Zionist Congress.
1904–1914 ▶	Second aliyah.

There was already a small community of Jews in Palestine, and a trickle of settlers had been arriving since the 1880s. Although only a minority of Jewish people chose to emigrate to Palestine, the Jewish population of the country rose from 24,000 in 1881 to 60–80,000 in 1914. However, the land, ruled by the Ottoman Empire, was already home to over 700,000 mostly Muslim Arabs.

This illustration shows Jews being attacked during a pogrom in Kiev, Russia, during the 1880s. The police fail to protect them.

CROSS-REFERENCE JEWISH SETTLEMENT IN PALESTINE: PAGES 8–11

The Jewish State

'Were I to sum up the Basle Congress in a word ... it would be this: At Basle I founded the Jewish State. If I said this out loud today, I would be answered by universal laughter. Perhaps in five years, and certainly in fifty, **everyone will know it.**'

Theodor Herzl, writing in his diary on 3 September 1897. Quoted in Martin Gilbert, *Israel: A History* (Doubleday, 1998).

Balfour Declaration

On 2 November 1917, British Foreign Secretary Arthur Balfour sent a letter to Lord Lionel Walter Rothschild, head of the British Zionist Federation. In this letter, known as the Balfour Declaration, the British government stated its support, in principle, for a Jewish homeland in Palestine.

VYING FOR POWER

At this time, Palestine was ruled by the Ottoman Empire. During World War I (1914–18), the Ottoman Empire was an enemy of Britain. Between 1914 and 1916, the British encouraged the Arabs of Palestine to help the Allies by rising up against their Ottoman rulers. In return, they made a vague promise that the Arabs might achieve independence after the war.

However, British views shifted. In early 1917 the Allies (France, Britain, Russia, Italy, Japan and, from April 1917, the USA) faced difficulties in the war against the Central Powers – mainly Germany, Austria-Hungary and the Ottoman Empire. In March 1917, the tsar gave up the Russian throne, and it became clear that his country, a key ally, would soon be out of the war. The British prime minister, David Lloyd-George, and his foreign secretary thought that Jewish people worldwide were extremely powerful and that they supported Zionism. Their views of the power and influence of worldwide Jewry were rather exaggerated. Yet they hoped that the declaration of support for a Jewish

Arthur Balfour on a visit to the USA in 1917. His Balfour Declaration had a huge influence on British policy towards Palestine.

homeland would rally Jewish support for the Allies – especially in the USA – and encourage Russian Jews to keep their nation in the war.

Another important factor motivating the British was the decline of the

---

British support for Zionism

'His Majesty's Government view with favour the establishment in Palestine of **a national home for the Jewish people**, and will use their best endeavours to facilitate the achievement of this object [do their best to achieve it], it being clearly understood that nothing shall be done which may prejudice [damage] the civil and religious rights of existing non-Jewish communities in Palestine, or the rights and political status enjoyed by Jews in any other country.'

Arthur James Balfour, Balfour Declaration, 1917.

CROSS-REFERENCE
BRITISH
INVOLVEMENT IN
PALESTINE: PAGES
8–11

TIMELINE

WORLD WAR I AND THE BALFOUR DECLARATION 1916–1920

9 May 1916 ▶ The Sykes-Picot Agreement between Britain and France defines the future division of the Ottoman Empire. Palestine is to come under international control.

15 March 1917 ▶ Tsar Nicholas II gives up his throne in Russia.

2 November 1917 ▶ Balfour Declaration.

December 1917 ▶ Jerusalem is captured by British and Allied forces.

October 1918 ▶ The rest of Palestine is captured by Britain.

11 November 1918 ▶ World War I ends, and an armistice agreement is signed.

19–26 April 1920 ▶ At the San Remo conference, the Allies divide up the territories of the former Ottoman Empire; Britain obtains a mandate over Palestine.

Ottoman Empire. Both France and Britain now hoped to claim Palestine after defeating the Central Powers in war. Through the Balfour Declaration, Britain wanted to show it was a protector of Jewish interests and had a right to a presence in the country.

STATEMENT OF SUPPORT

The Balfour Declaration was seen by the Zionist movement as a commitment to a Jewish homeland. The British had not consulted the Palestinian leaders over the declaration. They did not think they would be angry about it. It was not until February 1919 that a conference of leading Palestinians passed a resolution opposing the declaration. By this time, Britain had conquered Palestine. In 1920 the League of Nations (the international peacekeeping organization set up at the end of World War I) gave Britain a mandate over the country – the right to rule over Palestine until the League believed that the local people could rule themselves.

British forces, on the right, after their capture of Jerusalem in December 1917. They went on to capture the rest of the country and brought in military rule (rule by the army).

Arab Rebellion Begins

On 23 August 1929, several thousand Muslim Palestinians in Jerusalem attacked Jews in the streets and set shops alight. On the same day in Hebron, rioters broke into a yeshiva, a Jewish religious college, and murdered the only student there. The following day, they attacked Jewish homes and killed the inhabitants. The riots spread throughout the country. A week later, when British forces restored order, 133 Jews and 116 Arabs had lost their lives.

RELIGIOUS DISPUTE

The immediate cause of the riots was a conflict over control of the Western Wall, the holiest Jewish place. The Western Wall is the only surviving part of the Second Temple and forms part of the Temple Mount, the site of both ancient Jewish Temples. The Muslims call the area the Haram al-Sharif. It contains the Dome of the Rock and al-Aqsa mosque and is the third holiest place in Islam. The Muslims were in charge of the Western Wall, but some Jews demanded control over it.

Underlying the religious dispute were the fears of the Palestinians about the Yishuv, the Jewish community in Palestine. It had increased dramatically during the previous decade. In 1919 it formed less than 10 per cent of the population, but by 1931 it represented 20 per cent. In the 1920s, large areas of land were bought by the Yishuv.

ARAB REVOLT 1936–39

In the 1930s, land purchases increased. Many Arab tenant farmers lost their home and livelihood when landowners sold land to the Yishuv. The Arabs began to organize against the Zionists. In April 1936 a full-scale rebellion broke out, involving Palestinians at all levels of society. The political parties formed a united Arab High Committee, with prominent Palestinian leader Hajj Amin al-Husseini as its chair. The committee called for a general strike and the boycott of trade with the Yishuv. Rebel groups attacked Jewish settlements and British military bases. The rebellion continued until 1939, although the severe British response from 1937 – patrols, searches and the blowing-up of houses to flush out the rebels within – gradually weakened the movement.

British police questioning Palestinians after they were arrested for looting and violence during the riots of August 1929.

TIMELINE	ARAB REBELLIONS 1929–1936
14 August 1929	Jewish protesters in Tel Aviv call for their community to take control of the Western Wall.
23 August 1929	Muslim riots in Jerusalem begin
24 August 1929	Arabs riot in Hebron. The riots spread around the country.
21 October 1930	A British White Paper (government report) states that Jewish immigration should be limited.
14 February 1931	Britain reverses the 1930 White Paper.
30 January 1933	Adolf Hitler takes power in Germany, which causes a large increase in emigration of German Jews, including to Palestine.
April 1936	The Arab Revolt begins.

District	Arab (%)	Jewish (%)	Public and other (%)
Safed	68	18	14
Aka	87	3	10
Tabariyyah	51	38	11
An-Nasirah	52	28	20
Haifa	42	35	23
Jenin	83	1	16
Beisan	44	34	22
Nablus	86	1	13
Tulkarm	78	17	5
Yafa	47	39	14
Ramallah	98	1	1
Ar-Ramleh	77	14	9
Al-Quds	84	2	14
Gaza	75	4	21
Al Khalil	95	1	4
Bi'r As-Sabi'	15	1	84

CROSS-REFERENCE
PALESTINIAN RESISTANCE TO THE ESTABLISHMENT OF ISRAEL: PAGES 10–11

This map shows the districts of Palestine under the British Mandate. By 1945 Jews owned about one-third of the land in five districts: Tabariyyah, An-Nasirah, Haifa, Beisan and Yafa.

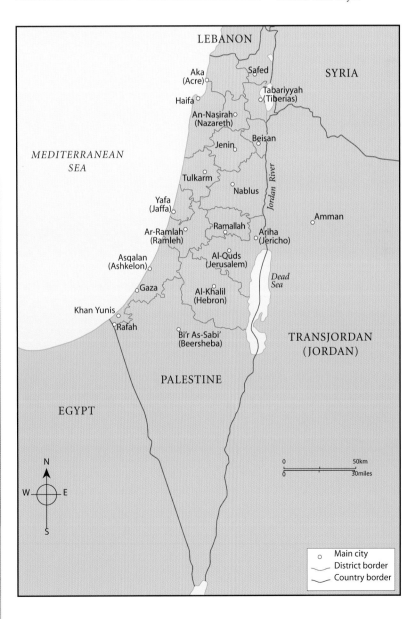

9

UN Partition Plan

On 29 November 1947, the United Nations (UN) partition plan proposed granting 55 per cent of Palestine to the Jewish people. A two-thirds majority in the UN was required for the plan to be accepted. At this time, soon after the Holocaust, during which six million Jews had perished at the hands of the Nazis, there was great sympathy internationally for the Jewish people. The USA realized that a Jewish state could be a useful ally in the Middle East. It campaigned for other countries to accept partition and threatened to withdraw aid from those that disagreed. A majority, although not the Arab countries, approved the plan.

BALANCING ACT

The British government had switched between supporting and discouraging the Zionists. In 1939, hoping to seek support from the Arab world in the forthcoming war with Germany, it issued a White Paper that restricted Jewish immigration to 75,000 a year during the next five years, limited Jewish land purchases and proposed an independent Palestinian state within 10 years. The White Paper angered the Yishuv. During World War II, Jewish people were desperate to escape from the Nazi Holocaust, but only relatively few could emigrate to Palestine.

After the war, the Yishuv was determined to fight for a state and began to focus attacks on the British.

Britain's attempts to achieve a peaceful solution failed, and in February 1947 it invited the UN to take over.

CIVIL WAR

The Palestinians did not agree with the partition plan. Upon its approval, civil war broke out in Palestine. The Palestinians had the upper hand in the civil war until April 1948, when the Haganah (the underground military organization of the Yishuv from 1920–1948) adopted Plan D. The aim was to secure all the territory allocated

Jewish refugees arriving in Palestine aboard the Exodus in 1947. At this time, Britain had a policy to limit Jewish immigration and sent the refugees back to Europe.

Deir Yassin, 9 April 1948

'...the conquest of the village was carried out with **great cruelty**. Whole families – women, old people, children – were killed, and there were piles of dead.'

Jewish commander Levy describes the mass killing of whole families in the Palestinian village of Deir Yassin, near Jerusalem, by two Jewish terrorist organizations, the Irgun and LEHI. The killings caused panic among Palestinians in general, and large numbers fled. Quoted in Benny Morris, *Righteous Victims: A History of the Zionist–Arab Conflict 1881–2001* (Vintage Books, 2001).

to the Zionists under the partition plan and to conquer further land to link it to the thirty-three Jewish settlements outside the proposed state. The Palestinians aimed to prevent this takeover. Casualties were heavy on both sides.

CROSS-REFERENCE
BRITISH INVOLVEMENT IN PALESTINE: PAGES 6–9
PALESTINIAN RESISTANCE TO THE ESTABLISHMENT OF ISRAEL: PAGES 8–9

April 1947: In their campaign against the British, Jewish terrorists blew up this train transporting British soldiers from Cairo to Haifa. Tens of thousands of Jews had fought for the Allies during the war and acquired military training, which they then put to use against their rulers.

Declaration of the State of Israel

On 14 May 1948, David Ben-Gurion, one of the leaders of the Yishuv, declared the establishment of the State of Israel. There was great celebration among the Zionists in the country and worldwide.

During the five-month civil war, the Yishuv had conquered far more land than it had been offered under the partition plan. By May 1948, large areas of land allocated to the Palestinians or to international control had been won. Hundreds of thousands of Palestinians in those areas, such as Jaffa and parts of Jerusalem, had been driven from their homes by Jewish fighters, were ordered to leave by Jewish forces, or were frightened into fleeing. The new State of Israel consisted of two connected north–south strips of the country, which were linked to each other. Plan D had succeeded.

Immigrants to Israel

Year	Number of immigrants
1948	101,828
1949	239,954
1950	170,563
1951	175,279
Source: Israel Ministry of Foreign Affairs	

INVASION

As dawn broke on 15 May, Egyptian planes attacked Tel Aviv. Armies from Egypt, Jordan, Syria, Lebanon and Iraq launched an invasion of the new State of Israel.

For Israel, this became known as the War of Independence. With five countries on their side, it seemed at first as if the Arabs had the advantage. Yet the Israelis were far more highly organized. The whole of society was mobilized – from new immigrants to foreign volunteers. They had more troops – perhaps 65,000 in July compared to about 40,000 Arab fighters.

The Arabs, on the other hand, did not make the most of their resources. Their forces were badly prepared and

Chaim Weizmann on a tour of inspection of a large Israeli army camp in November 1948, during the first Arab–Israeli war. Weizmann was a leading Zionist who became Israel's first president in 1949.

TIMELINE

INDEPENDENCE AND WAR 1947–1949

December 1947–March 1948	▶ Around 75,000 well-off Arabs flee Palestine.
April–June 1948	▶ Mass flight of Palestinians because of Zionist military attacks.
14 May 1948	▶ Establishment of Israel.
15 May 1948	▶ Invasion of Israel by five Arab armies.
July–November 1948	▶ About 300,000 Palestinians become refugees.
24 February 1949	▶ First armistice agreement between Israel and Egypt.
20 July 1949	▶ Final armistice agreement between Israel and Syria.

poorly coordinated. They suffered great shortages of weapons owing to an international arms embargo against the warring countries. Israel, however, had established secret arms deals in Europe and the Americas.

The war lasted until March 1949, and by July, Israel had signed armistice agreements (truces) with the Arab countries. Israel kept some areas newly occupied from the Palestinians, such as Ramla, Lydda and Beersheba. It now controlled 78 per cent of Palestine rather than the 55 per cent offered by the partition plan.

For the Palestinians, the war became known as the Naqba, the catastrophe. About half of their proposed state was incorporated into Israel. Jordan took the West Bank, including East Jerusalem, and Egypt acquired the Gaza Strip. They were left with nothing. Around 750,000 Palestinians who had fled Israel became refugees in the West Bank, Gaza, Jordan, Lebanon and Syria.

JEWISH SETTLEMENT IN PALESTINE: PAGES 4–5, 8–11 OTHER ARAB–ISRAELI WARS: PAGES 14–19, 24–25, 28–29, 44–45

These Palestinian refugees arrived in Amman, Jordan, in March 1948. Unable to find shelter in a house or tent, they were forced to build their own shelter in the open air.

Suez–Sinai War Begins

On 26 July 1956, Egyptian President Gamal Abdel Nasser nationalized the Suez Canal, bringing it under Egyptian ownership. He stopped Israel from using the canal and the Straits of Tiran. Britain and France controlled the company that had owned the canal and were furious. Along with Israel, they planned to conquer it. On 29 October, Israeli troops swept into Egypt and occupied the Sinai Peninsula. Two days later, Anglo-French forces destroyed the Egyptian air force but they failed to take the Suez Canal. After the war, the international community made Israel return the Sinai Peninsula to Egypt, but Israel regained shipping rights in the Straits of Tiran.

The war broke out against a background of continuing hostility between Israel and the Arab states. Arab countries refused to trade or have any contact with Israel. Violent clashes occurred regularly along the borders between Israel and the West Bank and Gaza Strip. Between 1948 and 1956, about 200 Israeli civilians and dozens of soldiers were killed by Arab infiltrators – fighters who had sneaked into Israel. In response, the IDF (Israel Defence Forces) shot anyone who crossed the border and set up special units to carry out counter-attacks.

29 OCTOBER 1956

NASSER, THE ARAB HERO

In 1952 an army officer, Gamal Abdel Nasser, overthrew King Farouk. He

The battle plan

'Bourgès told me that a join operation was being planned between France and England to **maintain their rights in the Suez Canal...** He asked me, if Israel participated, how long would it take the force to reach the canal?'

Shimon Peres, Director of the Israeli Defence Ministry, recalls his discussion with French Defence Minister Maurice Bourgès-Maunoury the day after Nasser announced the nationalization of the Suez Canal. Quoted in Ahron Bregman and Jihan el-Tahri, *The Fifty Years War: Israel and the Arabs* (Penguin, 1998).

British troops in Port Said, Egypt, during the Anglo–French invasion of the Suez Canal area in November 1956. You can see an oil installation on fire in the background.

THE SUEZ–SINAI WAR 1952–1957

23 July 1952	Nasser's Free Officers group takes power in Egypt from the king.
18 April 1954	Nasser becomes prime minister of Egypt.
25 September 1955	Egypt makes an agreement to buy Soviet arms from Czechoslovakia.
26 July 1956	Nasser nationalizes the Suez Canal.
23–24 October 1956	Representatives of Britain, France and Israel meet in Sèvres, France, to plot their attack on Egypt.
29 October 1956	Israel attacks the Sinai Peninsula in Egypt.
31 October 1956	Anglo–French troops invade the Suez Canal area.
7 November 1956	A ceasefire comes into effect.
6–8 March 1957	Israeli withdrawal from the Sinai Peninsula is completed.

was determined to strengthen Egypt and free it from foreign influence. From 1954, Nasser's army sent *fedayeen* ('self-sacrificers') to retaliate against Israeli attacks in the Gaza Strip. In 1954 he secured an agreement that Britain would withdraw its troops from military bases in the Suez Canal. The following year, Nasser made a deal to buy a huge quantity of weapons from Czechoslovakia. These developments raised fears in Israel of another Arab invasion and motivated the country to join Britain and France in the Suez–Sinai war.

Although Israel succeeded in occupying the Sinai Peninsula, Nasser emerged a hero among Arabs for standing up to Israel. He and other Arab leaders began to speak about a 'third round' of the war, in which the state of Israel would be destroyed.

Egyptian President Gamal Abdel Nasser is cheered by crowds in Cairo after announcing he had taken the Suez Canal Company into Egyptian hands.

CROSS-REFERENCE OTHER ARAB–ISRAELI WARS: PAGES 12–13, 16–19, 24–25, 28–29, 44–45

Six-Day War Begins

On 5 June 1967, the IDF made a surprise attack on Egyptian airfields and destroyed their planes. They moved ground forces into the Sinai desert, defeated Egypt's army and conquered the Gaza Strip and Sinai Peninsula. On the same day, Jordan attacked Israel and lost the West Bank. On 9 June Israel seized control of the Golan Heights from Syria. It was a spectacular Israeli victory.

WHY WAR?

Although there was great hostility between Israel and the Arab states in 1967, no country appeared to want war at this time. Around 70,000 of Egypt's soldiers were involved in a civil war in Yemen, and the other Arab states were unlikely to fight Israel without Egypt. Israel did not seek war. However, there is evidence that the Soviet Union and the USA were using the countries that depended on them for economic and military support to try to increase their own political power. In the Middle East, the Soviet Union backed Egypt and Syria; the USA supported Israel.

In May 1967, a Soviet minister warned the Egyptians that ten Israeli brigades had moved to the Syrian border. It was untrue. But the Soviet Union was keen to create a new trouble-spot for the USA, already fighting a war in Vietnam, and to show the world that Arab forces were fighting with Soviet weapons. President Nasser felt obliged to react to defend the Arab nations. He told the UN forces monitoring the

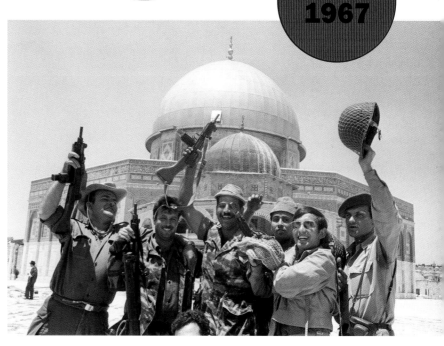

As a result of the 1967 war, the entire holy city of Jerusalem was in Jewish hands, including East Jerusalem, which had been under Jordanian rule. Here, Israeli soldiers celebrate the capture in front of the Dome of the Rock, one of the holiest Muslim sites.

Egypt–Israel border to leave and closed the Straits of Tiran to Israeli shipping. These actions provoked Israel. A difficult few weeks followed.

Israeli military occupation

- **The Palestinian economies, including utilities (electricity, water etc.) and transport, were linked to Israel's and controlled by it. Industrial development was prevented.**
- **Israelis took over land in the West Bank and Gaza Strip and built Jewish settlements.**
- **Political freedom was restricted, and there was strict censorship of the media.**
- **Punishments for protesting included curfew, house arrest (forcing people to stay at home), prison, expulsion, imprisonment without trial, school and workplace shutdowns.**

TIMELINE

THE SIX-DAY WAR 1967

12 May 1967	▶ The Soviet Union tells Egypt that Israel is building up forces along the Syrian border.
20–21 May 1967	▶ UN troops leave Sinai and Gaza; Egyptian troops take over.
24 May 1967	▶ Israeli ships are banned from the Straits of Tiran.
5 June 1967	▶ Israel attacks Egypt. Jordan attacks Israel. Israel attacks Syria.
10 June 1967	▶ Ceasefire.
22 November 1967	▶ UN adopts Security Council Resolution 242.

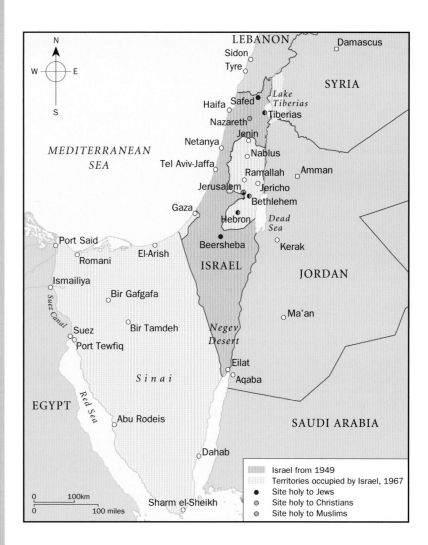

This map shows the new borders after the 1967 war. Israel greatly expanded the territory under its control.

The USA tried to prevent conflict, and the Soviet Union reversed its support for war and also attempted to stop it. However, tensions had risen too high for either side to back down, and Israel decided to act first.

OCCUPIED TERRITORIES

After this war, UN Security Council Resolution 242 was passed. It called for Israel to withdraw from the Occupied Territories in exchange for peace with the Arab states. However, it was not enforced, and 1.1 million Palestinians in the West Bank and Gaza Strip fell under the military rule of their enemy. Israel's occupation of these areas changed the face of the Arab–Israeli conflict.

CROSS-REFERENCE OTHER ARAB–ISRAELI WARS: PAGES 12–15, 18–19, 24–25, 28–29, 44–45

Battle of Karameh

On 21 March 1968, the IDF targeted Fatah bases around the village of Karameh, Jordan. They did not expect that Jordanians from a nearby Arab Legion force (part of the Jordanian army) would mount fierce resistance. The Jordanians fended off the Israeli tanks, many of which became stuck in wet ground, while Fatah fighters fought off the Israelis at Karameh. The IDF was forced to withdraw, and most of the guerrillas, including Yasser Arafat, managed to escape.

The resistance movement Fatah had been set up in Kuwait in 1959 by Arafat and other Palestinian exiles. From 1965, its guerrillas carried out attacks on Israeli civilians, launched from Jordan, Lebanon and Egyptian-ruled Gaza. Jordan and Egypt tried to clamp down on Fatah groups; they didn't want war with Israel before they were ready. Nevertheless, the raids continued.

Israel wanted to stop this low-level guerrilla war. On 18 March 1968 guerrilla fighters from Jordan blew

An Israeli soldier plants an explosive at an ammunition dump – a place where the IDF believed Fatah stored bullets and missiles.

up an Israeli school bus, killing two adults and wounding ten children. This led to a hasty, ill-prepared counter-raid at Karameh.

KARAMEH: TRUTH AND LEGEND

In reality, Karameh was not a huge military victory for Fatah – 156 of its fighters died and 141 were captured.

The PLO

The Palestine Liberation Organization (PLO) was set up in 1964 to bring together various Palestinian groups in one organization. Its declared goal was to destroy the State of Israel. The PLO became prominent after the 1967 war when it started to launch guerrilla attacks against Israel. The main group in the PLO was Fatah, and in 1969 Fatah leader Yasser Arafat became chairman of the PLO. The long guerrilla war with Israel lasted until the peace negotiations of the 1990s.

TIMELINE

THE PLO VERSUS ISRAEL 1964–1968

13–16 January 1964 ▶ The PLO is formed at an Arab summit meeting.

2 January 1965 ▶ Fatah's first raid into Israel, to blow up a water pump, is unsuccessful.

31 August 1967 ▶ Fatah attempts to launch a popular uprising in the Occupied Territories. It fails.

21 March 1968 ▶ IDF raids Karameh, in Jordan.

10 July 1968 ▶ The Palestinian National Charter, which lists the PLO's aims, states that 'armed struggle is the only way to liberate Palestine'.

The Arab Legion lost 84 lives and 350 were wounded. Israel suffered 33 dead and 161 wounded. However, although the Jordanians had played a significant role in the battle, Fatah was greatly boosted for standing up to the IDF. Thousands of young Palestinians rushed to join the movement. By the end of the 1960s, Fatah had taken control of the PLO (Palestine Liberation Organization).

Meanwhile, Israel stepped up its efforts to crush resistance in the Occupied Territories. Its soldiers controlled the movement of the Palestinians using road blocks, identity cards and travel permits. The Israeli secret service (known as Shin Bet) paid Palestinian spies (who became known as collaborators) to inform its agents about the Palestinian resistance. These tactics divided Palestinian society so that no one knew whom they could trust.

Young Palestinians in refugee camps grew up in an atmosphere of conflict. Some, like these boys, wanted to join Fatah's struggle against Israel as soon as they were old enough.

CROSS-REFERENCE OTHER ARAB–ISRAELI WARS: PAGES 12–17, 24–25, 28–29, 44–45

19

Black September

On 17 September 1970, the Jordanian army attacked the headquarters of Palestinian organizations in the capital Amman and the Palestinian refugee camps. The following day, Syria, the PLO's main supporter, invaded Jordan to protect the Palestinians. King Hussein of Jordan pleaded with the Americans for help to save his kingdom. US President Richard Nixon called on his Israeli allies to send forces to Jordan to frighten off the Syrians, which they did. Hussein now focused on defeating the Palestinians. Between 1,000 and 5,000 fighters and civilians were killed in a massive assault that became known as 'Black September'.

INSTABILITY IN JORDAN

During the late 1960s, King Hussein felt threatened by the growing power of the PLO in Jordan. The PLO was launching guerrilla raids on Israel from his country, which led to Israeli counter-attacks. Within the PLO, left-wing organizations called the Popular Front for the Liberation of Palestine (PFLP) and the Democratic Front for the Liberation of Palestine (DFLP) wanted to topple the Jordanian regime

The three aeroplanes blown up by PFLP fighters at Dawson's Field in the Jordanian desert. A war between the Jordanian army and the PLO followed.

Humiliation

'The humiliation of having aircraft flown into Jordan and innocent passengers being whisked away to various parts of the country, and being unable to do anything about it, and having the aircraft blown up, was something that questioned whether Jordan really existed. Well, **that was the limit.** As far as I was concerned, something had to be done – and done quickly.'

King Hussein explains an important reason behind Black September. Quoted in Ahron Bregman and Jihan el-Tahri, *The Fifty Years War: Israel and the Arabs* (Penguin, 1998).

CROSS-REFERENCE
PALESTINIAN
RESISTANCE
MOVEMENTS: PAGES
22–23, 30–31,
36–37, 38–39

TIMELINE

JORDAN VERSUS THE PLO 1970–1971

9 June 1970 ▶ Jordanians attack Palestinian refugee camps in Amman after guerrillas try to free *fedayeen* from a Jordanian prison.

10 July 1970 ▶ An agreement is made between the Jordanian government and the PLO, which soon breaks down.

30 August 1970 ▶ Jordanian army shells Fatah positions around Amman.

6 September 1970 ▶ PFLP hijacks three aeroplanes; most groups in the PLO oppose the hijacking. It blows up the aircraft six days later.

15 September 1970 ▶ Palestinian guerrillas take control of part of northern Jordan.

17 September 1970 ▶ The Jordanian army attacks the Palestinians.

27 September 1970 ▶ King Hussein signs a peace agreement with the PLO.

19 July 1971 ▶ King Hussein announces all PLO bases have been destroyed.

as well as Israel. The king was in a difficult situation because two-thirds of his population were Palestinians, and many sympathized with the PLO.

In May 1970, the antagonism between the Jordanian army and the PLO erupted into civil war. Hussein himself came under fire from guerrillas twice. On 6 September, the PFLP hijacked three planes and took them to Dawson's Field in Jordan. Although no one was hurt, the planes were blown up, and the incident attracted international attention. It seemed that Hussein was no longer in control of his country. He began a full-scale assault on the PLO. Ten days later, however, other Arab countries forced him to sign a peace agreement.

Determined to finish the job, the following April, Hussein ordered his troops to crush the Palestinian guerrillas, and by July most had been captured or had escaped. Many fighters shifted to Lebanon. Hussein's actions against the Palestinians were deeply unpopular among many Jordanians and in Arab countries.

Here, Fatah fighters surrender to the Jordanian army in July 1971, after King Hussein completely defeated the PLO in his country.

Killings at the Munich Olympics

It was the middle of the 1972 Munich Olympic Games. In the early hours of 5 September, Palestinian gunmen from the Black September organization stole into the athletes' dormitories in the Olympic Village and occupied the Israeli team's rooms. Two team members who tried to stop them were shot dead, while nine were taken hostage. During a rescue attempt, the West German police opened fire on the gunmen, who promptly killed all the athletes. Five terrorists and a policeman also died.

The purpose of the Munich action was to trade Israeli hostages for the release of about 200 Palestinians from Israeli prisons. Militants within the Palestinian movement favoured terrorist actions against Israeli and pro-Israeli Western states to try to advance their cause. In 1968 they adopted hijacking as a political tactic. On 23 July 1968, members of the PFLP hijacked an Israeli plane. They released the hostages in exchange for the freedom of 15 jailed Palestinians. From 1968–70, the PFLP carried out most Palestinian attacks abroad.

BLACK SEPTEMBER

In 1971, after the PLO was wiped out in Jordan, a small, secretive military organization was set up by Fatah. Called Black September in memory of the events of 1970 in Jordan, it carried out most Palestinian attacks on Israeli targets abroad in 1971–3. Its stated aim was 'to make the world feel that the Palestinian people exists'.

REACTIONS

After the Munich killings, the IDF immediately bombed PLO bases in Lebanon and Syria, killing or wounding about 200 Palestinians. Israel stepped up the protection of its institutions and citizens abroad and carried out counter-terrorist measures against the PFLP and Black September. Israeli Prime Minister Golda Meir set up a Mossad (intelligence agency) hit team to hunt down and kill their officers.

As a result of the Munich killings and other terrorist attacks, international

Armed police in Munich dropping into position above the apartments where the Israeli Olympic team members were being held hostage.

CROSS-REFERENCE
PALESTINIAN
RESISTANCE
MOVEMENTS: PAGES
20–21, 30–31,
36–37, 38–39

TIMELINE	PALESTINIAN TERROR 1968–1973
1968–1969	PFLP carries out most Palestinian attacks abroad.
June 1970	PFLP actions are directed against Jordan and the USA.
August 1971	Salah Khalaf begins to set up the Black September organization.
1971–1973	Greatest number yet of terrorist attacks by Palestinians abroad.
8 July 1972	Israeli agents in Beirut kill PFLP spokesman, the writer Ghassan Kanafani, and his 17-year-old niece.
5 September 1972	Black September assault on Israeli athletes at Munich Olympics.
9 April 1973	Mossad operation to kill PLO officers in Beirut.

sympathy for Israel grew. For the Palestinians, the campaigns focused world attention on the failure to solve the Arab–Israeli conflict, but the violent tactics undermined support for their cause. In 1973 the PLO decided that terrorism abroad was not the best way forward and it closed down Black September.

Yasser Arafat, chairman of the PLO, at a meeting of Arab leaders in 1974. Worldwide, he was the most famous figure in the Palestinian struggle and remained so until his death in 2004.

Palestinian military organizations

- **Black September: Set up in 1971 by Salah Khalaf, a founding member of Fatah, to attack Israeli targets abroad and undermine relations between Arab and Western governments.**
- **Fatah: Founded in 1959 by Yasser Arafat and Khalil al-Wazir to wage guerrilla war in an attempt to regain control of Palestine from the Israelis.**
- **Popular Front for the Liberation of Palestine (PFLP): Established in 1967 by George Habash. It rejected political compromise with Israel and organized many terrorist attacks against Israeli and Western interests.**

Yom Kippur War Begins

In position five days before the start of the Yom Kippur War, an Egyptian soldier holds up a portrait of President Anwar al-Sadat. The Egyptian army hoped that this time Israel would be defeated.

On 6 October 1973 – the Jewish holiday of Yom Kippur – Syria and Egypt launched a surprise attack on Israel, hoping to regain the territory they had lost in 1967. Most of the Israeli population was at prayer. Suddenly sirens went off, and radio broadcasts in code ordered soldiers to join their units.

During the first few days, Egyptian missiles attacked Israeli warplanes, and troops moved into Israeli-occupied Sinai. Israel called on the USA for military aid, and the IDF turned the tide. It disabled Egypt's air defences and threatened to destroy the Egyptian Third Army. On the Golan Heights, the IDF pushed back the Syrians and advanced towards Damascus. Under the threat of Soviet military intervention on the Arab side, the USA called for a ceasefire. By this stage about 12,000 Egyptians, 3,000 Syrians and 2,300 Israelis had died.

The attack on Israel

'When the time came, more than 200 planes flew from seven different airfields and 100 planes took off from Syria – each, one minute apart. They all flew very low until they crossed the Suez Canal Zone. At exactly 14.05 hours the aircraft were on target. We were all silent, focused on the radar. Then the first brigade crossed the canal and **put up the Egyptian flag** on the other side. We all cheered.'

General Abdel Ghani Gamasy, Egypt's military leader in 1973, remembers the attack on Israel. Quoted in Ahron Bregman and Jihan el-Tahri, *The Fifty Years War: Israel and the Arabs* (Penguin, 1998).

CROSS-REFERENCE
OTHER
ARAB–ISRAELI
WARS: PAGES
12–19, 28–29,
44–45
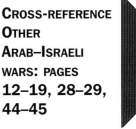

TIMELINE	**ARAB ATTACK** **1970–1974**
7 August 1970	▶ Ceasefire between Israel and Egypt to end the War of Attrition is immediately broken by Egypt.
15 October 1970	▶ Sadat becomes president following Nasser's death and does not continue the War of Attrition.
6 October 1973	▶ Egypt and Syria attack Israel.
22 October 1973	▶ The war officially ends when the UN Security Council calls for a ceasefire.
3 March 1974	▶ IDF completes withdrawal from the west bank of the Suez Canal, occupied during the war.
31 May 1974	▶ Agreement between Syria and Israel; Israel withdraws from territory conquered during the war and a strip of the Golan Heights.

There had been low-level warfare between Israel and Egypt in 1969–70, known as the War of Attrition (wearing down). President Nasser wanted to wear down Israel's defences on the Israeli–Egyptian border on the east bank of the Suez Canal, territory he hoped to return to Egypt. After some exchanges of fire in 1968, in March 1969 the Egyptians attacked Israeli forces on the border. In response, the IDF carried out air raids deep into Egypt. Between the Six-Day War and mid-August 1970, 367 Israelis died on the Egyptian front. The ability to inflict such high casualties gave new Egyptian president Anwar al-Sadat the confidence to go to Syria and propose war.

EGYPT'S NEW POSITION

Although Egypt and Syria lost the war, by catching Israel by surprise and crossing the Suez Canal, Egypt had won an important battle. Israel no longer appeared invincible. From this position of strength, Sadat decided to make peace with Israel, and many Israelis started to accept the need for peace with the Arab nations. But Israel still had the Occupied Territories, and most Arab countries were not prepared to come to terms with the Jewish state.

The remains of Syrian tanks, destroyed by the Israeli Air Force during the October 1973 war. After the war, the Soviet Union was quick to resupply Egypt and Syria with new tanks and guns, while the USA flew military supplies to Israel.

Camp David Accords with Egypt

On 26 March 1979, Israel signed a peace agreement with Egypt. The agreement permitted economic, diplomatic and cultural relations between the two countries, and enabled Israeli ships to pass through the Suez Canal. Israel agreed to return the Sinai to Egypt and dismantle Jewish settlements there. Israel kept control of the West Bank and Gaza Strip but said that it would allow the Palestinians self-rule.

The peace process began with a remarkable visit to Israel by President Sadat in November 1977. The first Arab leader to visit the Jewish state, Sadat spoke in the Knesset and called for peace. He hoped to avoid further conflict and allow economic links between the two countries. The subsequent negotiations proved complex. The Israeli government would not agree to a key Egyptian demand – reflecting general opinion in the Arab world – to restore the Occupied Territories to Arab rule. (Jordan retained its claim over the West Bank until 1988.) The Israeli people were divided. Some believed that these territories formed part of the biblical Land of Israel and were therefore Israel's by right. Others campaigned for Israel to give up the land in return for peace. In summer 1978, US President Jimmy Carter hosted talks between President Sadat and Israeli Prime Minister Menachem Begin at Camp David, USA, in an attempt to break the deadlock between them.

PEACE AT A PRICE

In the end, Egypt was willing to come to an agreement with Israel that did not include the requirement to hand back the Occupied Territories. Begin was pleased. He was from the right-wing Likud Party, which strongly believed that Israel should keep the West Bank and Gaza Strip. During the summer and autumn of 1979, Israel established new settlements in the West Bank and planned more in the Gaza Strip. War had become less likely because Egypt, the strongest neighbouring country, would no longer fight Israel.

President Sadat of Egypt speaking in the Israeli Knesset in November 1977. On his left is Yitzhak Shamir, who later served as Israeli prime minister in the 1980s and early 1990s.

TIMELINE

ISRAELI–EGYPTIAN PEACE 1977–1982

19 November 1977 ▶ President Sadat visits Israel.

5 September 1978 ▶ Talks begin between Carter, Sadat and Begin at Camp David.

17 September 1978 ▶ Framework peace agreement is signed, the basis of the peace agreement between Egypt and Israel.

26 March 1979 ▶ Peace agreement is signed by Sadat, Begin and Carter.

6 October 1981 ▶ Sadat is murdered.

25 April 1982 ▶ Israeli withdrawal from the Sinai is completed.

Number of Israeli settlers living in the West Bank*

Year	Number of settlers
1977 (May)	4,000
1978	7,500
1979	10,000
1980	12,500
1981	16,000

* excluding Jerusalem area

Sadat was content too. He had won back Sinai and rid his country of the burden of conflict. But the Arab states were incensed; all but Oman and Sudan broke off relations with Egypt – although relations were restored over the following decade. The Palestinians felt Sadat had abandoned them. The failure to return the Occupied Territories ensured continued confrontation between the Palestinians and Israel.

Sadat paid for peace with his life. In 1981 he was assassinated by members of a radical Islamic organization that opposed the peace treaty with Israel.

Jewish settlers moving into the new settlement of Elon Moreh in 1979, in the West Bank. When the Likud Party came to power in 1977, there were about 4,000 Jewish settlers in the West Bank; by 1981, the number had quadrupled to 16,000.

CROSS-REFERENCE PEACE PROCESS: PAGES 32–33, 34–35, 40–41, 42–43

Israeli Invasion of Lebanon

6 JUNE 1982

On 6 June 1982, Israel invaded Lebanon. It aimed to crush the PLO, remove the Syrian forces and install a Christian government that would make peace with Israel. The USA disagreed with the invasion but did nothing to halt it. For 70 days, the IDF besieged West Beirut, home to Palestinians and Muslim Lebanese as well as PLO fighters. The Lebanese government pleaded with Arafat to shift the PLO from Lebanon. Israel also inflicted serious damage on the Syrian forces. Although the figures are disputed, probably over 19,000 Arab military personnel and civilians, and 675 Israeli soldiers died in Lebanon before the USA-imposed ceasefire.

LEBANESE CIVIL WAR

There had been civil war between Christian forces and the Muslim Lebanese and Palestinians since 1975. Large numbers of Palestinian refugees lived in Lebanon, and the PLO was based there. In addition to the struggle within the country, PLO fighters launched raids on northern Israel from southern Lebanon, and Israel made counter-attacks. In 1976, the Lebanese government asked Syria to help stop the civil war. Israel did not want Syria to gain control of Lebanon and secretly began to back the Christian forces against their shared enemy, the PLO. In 1981, when Ariel Sharon became Defence Minister, he planned to invade Lebanon and destroy the PLO once and for all.

ISRAEL'S FAILED PLAN

Following the Israeli invasion, some of the PLO forces evacuated to Tunisia, far from the Palestinians in the Occupied Territories. Hezbollah, a new Islamic organization, was formed, with the aim of driving Israel out of Lebanon completely. In August 1982, Lebanese Christian leader Bashir Gemayel became president, as Israel had hoped. But the following month, Syrian agents assassinated him.

On the day of Gemayel's funeral, the Israelis permitted Christian troops to enter the Palestinian refugee camps of Sabra and Shatila to pursue remaining Palestinian fighters. Determined to

A march organized by Peace Now, the Israeli peace movement, in opposition to the invasion of Lebanon in 1982. The war divided Israeli society; some strongly supported it while others campaigned for peace with Israel's Arab neighbours.

CROSS-REFERENCE
OTHER ARAB–
ISRAELI WARS:
PAGES 12–19,
24–25, 44–45

TIMELINE	ISRAEL'S CAMPAIGN IN LEBANON 1978–1985
14–15 March 1978	Israel invades southern Lebanon to destroy PLO bases; the invasion ends in June.
3 June 1982	The attempted assassination of an Israeli ambassador in London provides the trigger for Israel to invade Lebanon.
4 June 1982	Israel starts bombing Lebanon.
6 June 1982	Around 60,000 Israeli troops invade Lebanon.
12 August 1982	USA achieves ceasefire; PLO agrees to leave Lebanon immediately.
14 September 1982	Syrian agents assassinate Bashir Gemayel.
14 February 1983	Sharon is forced to resign as defence minister.
June 1985	Israel completes its withdrawal but retains a 'security zone' in southern Lebanon.

avenge the death of Gemayel, although he had not been murdered by Palestinians, they massacred between 700 and 2,300 people.

In May 1983, Israel signed a treaty with Lebanon agreeing to withdraw its troops. Israel had failed to achieve its aims. Syria maintained an influence in Lebanon, and the PLO survived.

Destruction caused by the Israeli bombing of Beirut in June 1982. Following the horrendous massacres in Sabra and Shatila, the USA forced the IDF to withdraw from Beirut in September.

The massacres at Sabra and Shatila

'There were women lying in houses with their skirts torn up to their waists ... **children with their throats cut,** rows of young men shot in the back after being lined up at an execution wall. There were babies ... tossed into rubbish heaps alongside discarded US army ration tins, Israeli army equipment and empty bottles of whiskey.'

British journalist Robert Fisk describes the scene after the massacres at Sabra and Shatila. Quoted in www.countercurrents.org

Palestinian Intifada Begins

On 9 December 1987, tens of thousands of mourners attended the funeral in Gaza of four young men who had died in a road accident. A rumour spread that they had been murdered in revenge by relatives of an Israeli killed in Gaza. The following day, Palestinians demonstrated in Gaza and threw stones at soldiers. Israeli troops fired on the crowd, and an 18-year-old was shot dead. Now masses of unarmed protesters burst on to the streets of the Gaza Strip and the West Bank in an intifada – a popular uprising involving the whole of society. There were mass demonstrations, general strikes, a boycott of Israeli goods and refusals to pay taxes. The factions of the PLO set up a Unified National Leadership of the Uprising (UNLU) to coordinate the movement.

PALESTINIAN GRIEVANCES

The uprising broke out because Palestinians wanted to end the occupation and establish their own state. But Israel was seizing further land for Jewish settlements. By 1988, Israel had taken up to 55 per cent of land in the West Bank and 30 per cent of land in Gaza. Every day, more than 40 per cent of the Palestinian workforce travelled long distances to work for low pay in Israel. Most returned home to poverty and overcrowding in refugee camps. Rashad a-Shawa, former mayor of Gaza, said: 'People … are completely frustrated. They have lost hope that Israel will ever give them rights. They feel that the Arab states are incapable of achieving anything. They feel that the PLO, which they regard as their representative, failed to achieve anything.'

West Bank Palestinians in February 1988 during the early stage of the intifada. Men, women and children of all ages demonstrated. They had no firearms but threw stones at the soldiers, who did not know how to quell the protests.

TIMELINE

INTIFADA 1987–1993

9 December 1987	▶ Riots begin in the Gaza Strip.
January 1988	▶ IDF imposes curfews whenever trouble breaks out.
11 February 1988	▶ The radical Islamic movement Hamas is founded in the Occupied Territories.
March 1988	▶ UNLU calls on all West Bank and Gaza policemen to resign.
15 April 1988	▶ Abu Jihad, PLO leader helping to direct the intifada from Tunis, is killed by Mossad agents.
September 1993	▶ Intifada is called off.

ISRAELI RESPONSE

To try to stop the uprising, the IDF shot protesters, demolished the homes of organizers and arrested tens of thousands of Palestinians. Collective punishment was also used, such as sealing off villages from the outside world for weeks at a time. Around the world, Israel was seen as an aggressive force, pitched against powerless Palestinians.

The intifada ended with the peace agreement in 1993 (see pages 32–33). As well as many deaths, Palestinians in the Occupied Territories had suffered a drop in living standards of 35 per cent, owing to the conflict, strikes and shutdowns. They realized they could not end the occupation, while Israelis saw that the Palestinian issue had to be solved. The intifada focused international attention on the problem and led to renewed negotiations.

A Palestinian child plays in the dirt in Rafah refugee camp in the Gaza Strip, 1988. Many homes in the camps had no running water, and sewage ran in the streets.

CROSS-REFERENCE
PALESTINIAN RESISTANCE MOVEMENTS: PAGES 20–21, 22–23, 36–37, 38–39

Intifada deaths

Between December 1987 and December 1993:

- **1,110 Palestinians killed by Israeli security forces**
- **56 Israeli civilians killed in Israel**
- **58 Israeli civilians killed in Occupied Territories**
- **65 Israeli soldiers and police killed**

Source: B'tselem (Israeli human rights organization)

Oslo Accords

After the signing of the Oslo Accords, Israeli Prime Minister Yitzhak Rabin shakes hands with Palestinian leader Yasser Arafat while US President Bill Clinton looks on.

On 13 September 1993, Israeli Prime Minister Yitzhak Rabin and PLO leader Yasser Arafat signed the Oslo Accords. Arafat confirmed that the PLO recognized Israel's right to exist in peace and would no longer use violence against it. Rabin recognized the PLO as the representative of the Palestinians. A temporary Palestinian Authority was set up in the Occupied Territories to rule over the Palestinians for five years, until a permanent settlement could be reached.

IRAQ AND KUWAIT

The PLO had declared in 1988 that it was ready to accept a two-state solution: Israel within pre-1967 borders, and Palestine in the West Bank and Gaza Strip. In 1990, the issue was pushed to the forefront of world affairs after Iraq invaded and occupied neighbouring Kuwait, in the Persian Gulf. Iraqi ruler Saddam Hussein proposed that there should be a solution to all the occupations in the Middle East, including the Israeli occupation of Palestinian land. The PLO sided with Saddam Hussein, although several Arab countries opposed him.

In January–February 1991, a US-led international force defeated Iraq and ended its occupation of Kuwait. Owing to Arafat's backing for Iraq, he lost favour with the international community and, perhaps more importantly, support and funding from the Persian Gulf states. But US President George Bush promised that once the USA had 'liberated' Kuwait, it would return to the peace process.

THE OSLO CONNECTION

In 1991, a peace conference was held in Madrid with representatives from the countries involved in the Arab–Israeli conflict. Israel would talk only to Palestinians who were not in the PLO, arguing that the PLO was a terrorist organization. Nothing was

Watching Rabin and Arafat

'Rabin didn't want to shake Arafat's hand. It was terrible. The whole world was watching – and could see from Rabin's body language that **he did not want to look at Arafat.** Finally, though, Rabin shook his hand and Arafat, who is an expert in these matters, hung on to it.'

Israeli Foreign Minister Shimon Peres recalls the signing of the Oslo Accords. Quoted in Ahron Bregman and Jihan el-Tahri, *The Fifty Years War: Israel and the Arabs* (Penguin, 1998).

resolved, however. In June 1992, the Labour Party won the elections and Yitzhak Rabin became prime minister. He decided to pursue an agreement with the PLO. From January 1993, secret talks between the PLO and Israeli academics were held near Oslo in Norway. After several months, the talks were made public and became the official channel for negotiations. The Oslo Accords were the result.

Over the following three years, the Israelis withdrew their forces from Gaza and many West Bank towns and villages. There were high hopes for a peaceful solution.

CROSS-REFERENCE PEACE PROCESS: PAGES 26–27, 34–35, 40–41, 42–43

In July 1994, cheering crowds welcomed Yasser Arafat to Gaza, where he was to rule over the Palestinians in the West Bank and Gaza Strip. The territories remained under the overall control of Israel.

Assassination of Yitzhak Rabin

On 4 November 1995, nearly 100,000 Israelis attended a rally in Tel Aviv in support of the peace process. On the platform with Shimon Peres, Yitzhak Rabin was overjoyed at the turnout. After the rally, as he was leaving, a lone right-wing Jewish militant shot him dead.

WHY WAS RABIN MURDERED?

As Prime Minister (1992–5), Rabin negotiated the 1993 Oslo Accords and signed a peace treaty with Jordan in 1994. In September 1995, the Oslo II agreement was signed, which provided a timetable for the extension of self-rule in the West Bank. However, Israeli society was divided over the peace process. Many in the Labour Party and left-wing organizations thought Israel should continue to talk to the PLO and exchange land for peace. Yet the Likud and other right-wing parties did not accept that Israel should give up any territory to the Palestinians.

PALESTINIAN VIEWS

The Palestinians were also split. Like the Israeli right wing, the militant groups Hamas and Islamic Jihad aimed to stop the peace process. They did not believe it would deliver a Palestinian state. After the Oslo Accords, Israel still possessed 60 per cent of the West Bank and 40 per cent of the Gaza Strip, and controlled the land, water and security of those territories. Militants organized a wave of suicide bombings in Israeli cities, in what they saw as a war to win back Palestine.

Other Palestinians, who had initially supported the Oslo Accords, soon became disillusioned. After the

Yitzhak Rabin, right, singing a peace song with singer Miri Alonie and Shimon Peres at the peace rally in November 1995 at which he was shot dead.

Rabin's murderer, extreme right-winger Yigal Amir, who believed that his drastic action was necessary to try to stop the peace process.

RABIN AND AFTER 1994–1996

1 July 1994 ▶ Yasser Arafat enters Gaza.

5 July 1994 ▶ Arafat establishes the Palestinian Authority (PA), which takes control of Palestinian education, culture, health and welfare, and taxation.

26 October 1994 ▶ A peace treaty between Jordan and Israel is signed.

28 September 1995 ▶ Oslo II Agreement is signed.

4 November 1995 ▶ Rabin is assassinated.

20 January 1996 ▶ Arafat is voted head of the PA.

29 May 1996 ▶ Benjamin Netanyahu wins the elections in Israel.

The Oslo II Agreement, 28 September 1995

- IDF to withdraw from six main cities of the West Bank, except Hebron, and around 450 villages.
- A president and council of the Palestinian Authority to be elected to run civil services, such as health and education.
- Israel to retain overall control of land, water and security and rule the Jewish settlements in the West Bank and Gaza Strip.

signing of the peace agreement, 35 countries pledged $3.2 billion (£1.7 billion) to the Palestinian areas, but only a fraction of the money arrived. The Palestinian Authority (PA), which assumed control of civil services from 1994, was starved of funds to develop the region and improve people's lives. Within the PA, there was widespread corruption, which also held back development.

ISRAELI VIEWS

For a few months after Rabin's assassination, there was popular Israeli support for the peace process. The withdrawal from the West Bank towns under Oslo II took place peacefully. But in spring 1996 there were several devastating attacks by suicide bombers. Israelis feared for their safety, and support increased for the Likud Party, seen as tough on security. In May 1996, Benjamin Netanyahu of Likud was elected prime minister. Over the next few years, there was little progress in the peace process.

CROSS-REFERENCE PEACE PROCESS: PAGES 26–27, 40–41, 42–43

Al-Aqsa Intifada Breaks Out

On 29 September 2000, Palestinians demonstrated in East Jerusalem and the West Bank, and several protesters were shot dead by Israeli police. The following day, a 12-year-old Gazan boy was killed, caught in crossfire between Palestinian militants and Israeli troops. Riots and protests spread throughout the West Bank and the Gaza Strip, and drew in Palestinians within Israel too. On 12 October, two Israeli soldiers were captured and murdered by Palestinians in the West Bank city of Ramallah. A new intifada had broken out.

PROVOCATION

On 28 September, the leader of the Israeli opposition Likud party, Ariel Sharon, visited the Temple Mount in East Jerusalem, holy to both Muslims and Jews. Sharon intended to show that the 'Temple Mount is in our hands and will remain in our hands.' However, the Palestinians hoped that East Jerusalem could be the capital of a future Palestinian state. The visit clearly provoked them.

Tensions were already running high. The Palestinians were frustrated because less than one-fifth of the West Bank and two-thirds of the Gaza Strip had come under their full control. Over the past decade, the number of Israelis living in Jewish settlements in the West Bank had grown by about 80,000. On average, people had grown poorer since 1991. It was hard for Palestinians to travel for work or study because of curfews and checkpoints. In many ways, life was worse than before the peace process. Talks between Arafat and Labour Party Prime Minister Ehud Barak at Camp David, USA, in July 2000 had failed to break the deadlock over land, control of Jerusalem and the right of Palestinian refugees to return.

ISRAELI RESPONSE

Large numbers of Israeli voters decided that a tough leader was needed to defeat the intifada and bring security, and Likud leader Sharon was elected prime minister in February 2001. In this uprising, the Palestinians had guns,

Ariel Sharon (centre, wearing sunglasses) on his visit to the Temple Mount in September 2000, surrounded by bodyguards.

TIMELINE

**THE SECOND INTIFADA
2000–2001**

**16 June
2000** ▶ Israeli withdrawal
from 'security zone' in
Lebanon completed.

**11–15 July
2000** ▶ Camp David talks end
in failure.

**28 September
2000** ▶ Ariel Sharon visits the
Temple Mount.

**29 September
2000** ▶ Riots and protests
break out in the West
Bank.

**6 February
2001** ▶ Ariel Sharon wins the
Israeli elections and
becomes prime
minister.

**18 May
2001** ▶ Israel starts to use
F-16 jet fighter planes
to target Palestinian
militants in Gaza.

hand grenades and mortars. They attacked Jewish settlers as well as the IDF. The IDF used overwhelming force to try to crush them. It unleashed fighter jets, helicopter gunships and tanks against the Palestinian population, causing heavy casualties. Israel organized the assassination of leading militants from Hamas, Islamic Jihad and the Al-Aqsa Martyrs' Brigade, a newer organization. These groups were responsible for suicide bombings against Israeli civilians. Despite Israel's tough response, the intifada continued.

These Palestinians in Ramallah celebrated when they saw the blood of the two captured Israeli soldiers on the hands of their killers, October 2000.

**CROSS-REFERENCE
PALESTINIAN
RESISTANCE
MOVEMENTS: PAGES
20–21, 22–23,
30–31, 38–39**

A warning ignored

'If Sharon visits the Haram [Temple Mount] **there will be a crisis** and no one could control it … the people are tired … and [Sharon's visit] is a big excuse for [Palestinians] who [are] under pressure to react.'

Mohammed Dahlan, head of Preventive Security forces in Gaza, urged the Israeli government and the USA to stop Sharon from visiting the Temple Mount. Quoted in Ahron Bregman, *Elusive Peace* (Penguin Books, 2005).

'Operation Defensive Shield' Begins

On 29 March 2002, Israel launched 'Operation Defensive Shield', a full-scale invasion of the West Bank. The tanks rolled into the major cities, and the IDF seized control. Parts of Arafat's headquarters in Ramallah were destroyed, and he was placed under siege. A prime target of the operation was the refugee camp of Jenin, home to around 14,000 Palestinians and perhaps 200 militants. The army demolished the homes of suspected militants and bombarded the camp with tanks and missiles. Large numbers of Palestinian men were arrested. According to the Palestinian Red Crescent, at least 216 Palestinians and 29 Israelis died during the operation.

ATTEMPTS TO CURB TERROR

The cycle of violence had been continuing relentlessly. Palestinian militants carried out suicide bombings, and Israeli forces assassinated the organizers. Sharon's government put pressure on Arafat to curb terrorist activities, but many Israelis believed he was involved in them.

In reality, Arafat's government was probably too weak to control the movements that engaged in violent resistance. He may have felt that the suicide bombings increased the pressure on Israel to leave the West Bank and Gaza Strip. However, after the terrorist attacks on the USA of 11 September 2001 and the new US campaign to wipe out terrorism worldwide, there was even more pressure on Arafat to halt Palestinian militants.

Karine A AFFAIR

A few months later, the *Karine A* affair indicated to Israel that Arafat was not serious about ending Palestinian violence. In January 2002, the Israeli navy captured the *Karine A*, which was bound for Gaza. On board the ship was 50 tonnes of weaponry, including rockets and anti-aircraft missiles. Under the Oslo Accords, the Palestinians were allowed only small weapons. Israel was convinced Arafat was involved in the secret arms purchase. Sharon decided that if Arafat would not control terrorism, Israel would have to do it.

Two Palestinians amid the rubble in Jenin refugee camp after the Israeli invasion of March–April 2002. During the attacks, the IDF used giant bulldozers to clear a path for the tanks, destroying many homes.

TIMELINE

ASSASSINATIONS AND WEST BANK INVASION 2001–2002

17 October 2001	▶ PFLP kills far-right Israeli minister Rehavam Zeevi.
3 January 2002	▶ The *Karine A* is captured.
27 March 2002	▶ Suicide bombing in Netanya.
29 March 2002	▶ Israel launches 'Operation Defensive Shield'.
21 April 2002	▶ 'Operation Defensive Shield' ends.
2 May 2002	▶ Siege of Arafat's headquarters ends.
10 May 2002	▶ Siege of Church of the Nativity ends.

The trigger for 'Operation Defensive Shield' was a suicide bombing in the Israeli town of Netanya in March. It killed 29 and wounded nearly 150. Sharon planned to recapture the West Bank towns, where, unlike Gaza, there was no barrier to stop terrorists crossing into Israel.

The Israelis ended the operation and withdrew their forces on 21 April. However, believing that they had not yet achieved their aims, in mid-June, they launched 'Operation Determined Path' and reoccupied most of the West Bank for several months.

On 2 April 2002, Palestinian militants sought refuge in the Church of the Nativity in Bethlehem. The Israelis placed the church under siege, only lifting it when most of the militants agreed to go to Gaza.

CROSS-REFERENCE PALESTINIAN RESISTANCE MOVEMENTS: PAGES 20–21, 22–23, 30–31, 36–37

Jenin

'This is horrifying beyond belief... it looks like there's been an earthquake here, and the stench of death is over many places where we are standing... No military operation could justify the suffering we are seeing here.'

UN envoy Terje Roed-Larsen describes Jenin refugee camp after the battle. Quoted in Ahron Bregman, *Elusive Peace* (Penguin Books, 2005).

Roadmap for Peace

On 30 April 2003, the Quartet (the USA, European Union, Russia and the UN) released the roadmap for peace. The Palestinians were to hold democratic elections and end terrorism. Israel was to withdraw from the Palestinian areas occupied since the start of the intifada and freeze the expansion of Jewish settlements. Then the borders of a Palestinian state would be roughly defined. Finally, agreements would be reached on the status of Jerusalem, Palestine's borders, the fate of Jewish settlements and the right of Palestinian refugees to return.

REASONS FOR THE ROADMAP

By 2003, nearly 2,300 Palestinians and around 575 Israelis had died in the al-Aqsa intifada. Economic activity in the Palestinian areas had virtually ceased because of curfews to stop the movement of terrorists. In Israel, the economy suffered too, and unemployment reached a new high of over 10 per cent.

The USA had an important influence on the roadmap. US President George W. Bush had promised to restart the peace process after the war with Iraq in 2003. But he now believed Arafat was too deeply involved in terrorism to achieve peace. Sharon also blamed Arafat for failing to stop suicide bombings and refused to negotiate with him. The USA and Israel decided a new Palestinian leadership was needed. Arafat was persuaded to

Israel hoped that agreement to the roadmap could stop Palestinian suicide bombings, like this one in northern Israel in October 2002, which left 14 people dead.

The Separation Barrier

- Length: 700 km.
- Route: mostly through the West Bank on Palestinian land.
- Palestinians affected (April 2006): nearly 500,000 (247,800 east of the barrier – they are either completely or partially surrounded by the barrier; 27,520 west of the barrier – they leave their homes through a gate in the barrier).
- Thousands of Palestinian farmers experience difficulty reaching their fields owing to restrictions on crossing from one side to the other.

appoint Mahmoud Abbas (known as Abu Mazen) as prime minister, while he would remain as president.

ROAD TO NOWHERE?

Although both sides accepted the roadmap, neither side complied with it.

THE ROADMAP AND CEASEFIRE 2002–2003

19 September 2002	▶ IDF besieges Arafat's compound for 10 days.
30 April 2003	▶ Palestinian Prime Minister Mahmoud Abbas and his cabinet take office. The roadmap is released.
26 June 2003	▶ The Gaza Agreement: Israel transfers security in the Gaza Strip and Bethlehem area to the PA.
28 June 2003	▶ Hamas, Islamic Jihad and Tanzim (militants linked to Fatah), but not Al-Aqsa Martyrs' Brigade, agree to a three-month ceasefire with Israel.
14 August 2003	▶ Israel breaks the ceasefire to assassinate Mohammed Seder, head of Islamic Jihad's armed wing in Hebron.
19 August 2003	▶ Hamas avenges the assassination with a suicide bombing in Jerusalem, killing 23.
6 September 2003	▶ Mahmoud Abbas resigns.

A ceasefire between Israel and Palestinian militants proved short-lived. Abu Mazen could neither prevent the terrorist groups from carrying out actions against Israel nor improve Palestinian social and economic conditions. He resigned in September.

Israel continued to build settlements and to construct a separation barrier (started in 2002) between Israel and the West Bank to stop suicide bombers crossing into Israel.

CROSS-REFERENCE PEACE PROCESS: PAGES 26–27, 32–33, 34–35, 42–43

The construction of the Separation Barrier around Qalqilya in the West Bank, 2003. The wall has cut off the residents, mostly farmers, from their land. Few people are allowed to enter, so it is hard for friends and family to visit, and local businesses have been destroyed.

Israeli civilians killed by Palestinians in Israel, 2000–2005

Year	Number killed
2000	4
2001	85
2002	184
2003	104
2004	53
2005	24

Source: B'tselem

Disengagement from Gaza Begins

On 15 August 2005, the IDF began to dismantle all 21 settlements in the Gaza Strip and 4 West Bank settlements. Despite strong opposition to the move from the 9,000 Jewish settlers and their supporters in Israel, the predicted violent clashes between the army and settlers did not occur. Within one week, all the settlers had left.

LEAVING GAZA

Sharon wanted to give back the Gaza Strip to the Palestinians and rid Israel of responsibility for 1.4 million Palestinians in a desperately poor region. Yet he intended to strengthen control over the West Bank, ensuring that the Jewish settlements there would become part of Israel in any future peace agreement. Many Palestinians welcomed the withdrawal plan but called for Israel to leave the West Bank too. The settlers and their supporters disagreed with the move, arguing that 'Jews don't expel Jews'.

WEAKENING HAMAS

After announcing his disengagement plan in 2003, Sharon was determined to seriously weaken Hamas before the Israeli troops left. The security forces carried out a concerted campaign to wipe out its leadership. Then, in

A Jewish settler and her child, forced to leave the Gaza settlement of Neve Dekalim in August 2005.

Expelled

'The past couple of weeks have seemed like years. We were expelled from our community and relocated... Not all have adjusted to new, smaller quarters. Many of the houses are too small to accommodate a whole family so some families have been split up. There are **so many individual stories to tell about frustrations** with re-establishing businesses... Others, unemployed for the first time in years, are looking for work... All the frustrations of a new life, but not one embarked on by choice.'

Pesach Aceman, a Jewish settler in Gaza forced to leave in 2005, writing in his diary about his experience. Reported on BBC News, 2 September 2005.

November 2004, Arafat died, which changed the situation. Mahmoud Abbas, the new PA president, was seen as more likely to negotiate with Israel. In February 2005 he and Sharon agreed a ceasefire to end the intifada. Most radical militias observed the ceasefire, although a few attacks still occurred. Nevertheless, the disengagement plan was a unilateral act by Israel – carried out without Palestinian agreement.

AFTERMATH

After the disengagement, the PA ruled in Gaza, yet Israel still controlled its airspace and access to the territory by sea and land. The PA claimed that Gaza was still occupied because it did not form part of an independent country, although Israel disagreed. At the international level, the disengagement brought Israel higher standing, and its ties with the USA became even closer. Gaza's situation didn't change much, however. Little of the investment money promised by other nations arrived, and there were few signs of economic improvement.

CROSS-REFERENCE PEACE PROCESS: PAGES 26–27, 32–33, 34–35, 40–41

After the settlers had left, the settlements in the Gaza Strip were destroyed. The Israelis did not want their homes taken over by Palestinians, and the Palestinians needed the land to develop industry and agriculture as well as new housing.

Israel–Lebanon War Begins

12 July 2006

On 12 July 2006, following Hezbollah rocket attacks on Israel and the kidnap of two Israeli soldiers, the IDF began a bombing campaign in Lebanon and invaded the country. In response, Hezbollah fired hundreds of rockets at civilian targets in northern Israel. A month later, the IDF was forced to withdraw from Lebanon.

HEZBOLLAH

Hezbollah was formed in 1982 in Lebanon to combat the Israeli invasion. Its stated aim was to destroy the State of Israel. Hezbollah has had violent clashes with Israel ever since. After the Israeli withdrawal from Lebanon of 2000, it became a leading political party and provided social services for the Lebanese as well as fighting Israel. In most Arab and Muslim countries, Hezbollah was regarded as a resistance movement, while Israel and some Western countries saw it as a terrorist organization linked to the Islamic regime of Iran. Israel was determined to crush it. The trigger for the war came in July 2006, with the kidnap of two Israeli soldiers by Hezbollah.

HEZBOLLAH VICTORY?

According to some observers, Hezbollah won the war. It had defended itself in the face of massive air and land attacks from Israeli forces. Israel and the USA declared that Hezbollah had lost, because

August 2006: An Israeli police officer orders civilians to keep out of the way after a Hezbollah rocket landed in the northern city of Haifa. More than 250 rockets were fired by Hezbollah just before the UN ceasefire came into effect.

Issues to be resolved

For Israel
- security from attack from Palestinian areas and peace with neighbouring Arab countries
- secure borders
- continued control over the holy city of Jerusalem.

For the Palestinians
- an independent state under their complete control, with East Jerusalem as the capital
- an end to Jewish settlements on the West Bank
- the right of refugees to return to their homeland.

hundreds of its fighters were killed, and it was forced to withdraw from southern Lebanon, to be replaced by a Lebanese and international force. The conflict caused huge casualties and massive destruction. Over 1,000 Lebanese lost their lives, mostly civilians, and there was extensive damage to the buildings, roads, bridges and power supplies across the country. An estimated 44 Israeli civilians and 119 soldiers were killed.

ISRAEL AND GAZA

Meanwhile, conflict between Israel and the Palestinians continued after Israel withdrew from Gaza. Israel fired artillery shells into Gaza; Palestinians launched missile attacks in return.

In January 2006, Hamas won the elections to the PA, defeating Fatah. Israel saw Hamas as a terrorist organization that would not pursue the peace process. Then in June, following kidnaps by both sides, Israeli forces entered Gaza, captured Hamas government members and carried out air strikes. Between 25 June and the end of August 2006, nearly 200 Palestinians were killed in air raids and ground assaults, and there was major damage to roads, bridges and government buildings.

CROSS-REFERENCE OTHER ARAB–ISRAELI WARS: PAGES 12–19, 24–25, 28–29

This Lebanese family returned to their home, destroyed by Israeli bombs in the war of July–August 2006. Despite the ceasefire, Israel was still bombing near their village, so they packed to leave once again.

Key Figures in the Arab–Israeli Conflict

PRESIDENT MAHMOUD ABBAS (1935–)

Mahmoud Abbas, also known as Abu Mazen, was one of the founding members of Fatah. Seen by Israel as devoted to achieving peace, he headed the Palestinian negotiating team at the secret Oslo talks and signed the 1993 Oslo Accords on behalf of the PLO. In April 2003 Abbas was elected the first prime minister of the Palestinian Authority (PA). Yet Arafat would not give him authority over security services and Israel did not make moves towards peace that would have brought him the support of his people. He resigned after four months. Following Arafat's death, Abbas was elected president of the PA in January 2005.

YASSER ARAFAT (1929–2004)

Born to a Palestinian family, Yasser Arafat helped to found Fatah and in 1969 became PLO chairman. In 1971 the PLO was expelled from Jordan and moved its operation to Lebanon. The Israeli invasion of Lebanon in 1982 forced the PLO to move again, to Tunisia. In 1993 Arafat signed the Oslo Accords with Israel. He moved to Gaza the following year and was elected president of the Palestinian Authority in 1996. Israeli Prime Minister Ariel Sharon blamed Arafat for involvement in terror attacks on Israel, and during IDF invasions of the West Bank in 2002, Arafat was twice besieged in his headquarters. He died of an unexplained illness in 2004.

DAVID BEN-GURION (1886–1973)

David Ben-Gurion was born in the Russian Empire. He emigrated to Palestine aged 20 and joined the struggle to establish a Jewish state. After World War I broke out, the Ottoman rulers of Palestine expelled him for his Zionist activities, but he returned after the Balfour Declaration of 1917 promised a national homeland for the Jews. In 1920 he founded the Histadrut and a decade later the Israeli Workers Party. Ben-Gurion was elected chairman of the Zionist Executive, the most important worldwide Zionist organization, in 1935. Following the 1939 White Paper, he called on Jewish people to fight the British to achieve their state. In 1948 he became the first prime minister of Israel, a position he held until 1953 and from 1955–63.

KING HUSSEIN OF JORDAN (1935–99)

Hussein ibn Talal became King of Jordan in 1953, aged 18. He had close ties to the USA and received aid to build up his military forces. His defeat by Israel in the 1967 war was a huge setback and Jordan lost the West Bank to Israel. In the late 1960s, Hussein's rule was threatened by the power of the PLO, which was based in Jordan, and in 1971 he completely expelled the organization. In 1988, he surrendered Jordan's claim to the West Bank to the PLO. In 1994 King Hussein signed a peace treaty with Israel.

HAJJ AMIN AL-HUSSEINI (1897–1974)

Born in Jerusalem, in 1921 al-Husseini was made president and mufti (leader) of the Palestinian Muslim community by the British rulers of Palestine. He came to dominate the Palestinian Arab movement against the Zionists. In 1936 al-Husseini became the chair of the Arab High Committee, which coordinated the Arab Revolt of 1936–9. The British removed him from the position of mufti, and in 1937 he fled to Lebanon, where he continued to lead the Arab High Committee. He supported Adolf Hitler's Nazi regime and in 1941 moved to Germany. At the end of World War II, he fled to Egypt.

GOLDA MEIR (1898–1978)

Golda Meir's family moved to the USA from the Ukraine in 1906, and in 1921 Golda emigrated to Palestine. Meir became an official of the Histadrut in 1924. During the war of 1947–9, she fundraised in the USA to help cover Israel's costs. She became a Knesset member in 1949 and foreign minister in 1956. Meir helped to strengthen Israel's relationship with the USA and forged relations with Latin American countries. In 1969 she became prime minister. After the Yom Kippur War of 1973, an enquiry concluded that the IDF and the government had made serious mistakes in failing to predict the war. Although the Labour Party won the elections of December 1973, Meir resigned in 1974.

GAMAL ABDEL NASSER (1918–70)

Born in Alexandria, Egypt, Gamal Abdel Nasser joined the army as a young man. In 1952 he and 89 other officers staged a coup against the king, and in 1954 he named himself prime minister. In 1956 he became president. The same year, he announced the nationalization of the Suez Canal, which led to an invasion by Israel, France and Britain. Nasser built the Aswan High Dam to control the annual floods, promoted the growth of industries and broke up large landholdings to provide land for poor farmers. But there was no freedom to disagree with the government: from 1962 Nasser's Arab Socialist Union was the only legal political party. After defeat in 1967 (Six-Day War), Nasser almost resigned, but popular support persuaded him to stay in office.

ARIEL SHARON (1928–)

Ariel Sharon was born in Palestine. He joined the Haganah at the age of 14 and fought in the 1947–9 war. He served in the army after Israel was founded and fought in the wars of 1956, 1967 and 1973. Sharon served in the Begin government of 1977–81 and was appointed defence minister in 1981, initiating the war against Lebanon of 1982. Sharon served as a minister in various governments during the 1980s and 1990s, and as leader of the right-wing Likud party was elected prime minister in 2001. In 2005, he withdrew all Jewish settlers and soldiers from Gaza. After suffering a stroke in December 2005, his duties were passed on to Ehud Olmert.

Glossary

Al-Aqsa Martyrs' Brigade Palestinian militant group linked to Fatah that began to attack Israeli civilians in 2002

anti-Semitism hatred of Jews because of their religion or race

boycott organized effort to weaken a group or a country by refusing to buy from or trade with it

censorship banning of newspapers, TV and radio programmes or other media that a government thinks could damage its interests

commando unit military unit trained and organized to carry out hit-and-run raids into enemy territory

counter-terrorism actions taken to try to prevent terrorist attacks

curfew rule requiring people to be indoors during certain hours

embargo official suspension of commerce (buying and selling)

exile someone who is forced to live outside their home country

fedayeen members of an Arab commando unit carrying out actions against Israel

guerrilla person in an independent fighting unit, not a regular army, that carries out attacks on the enemy

Haganah underground military organization of the Yishuv, 1920–48

Hamas militant Palestinian Islamic movement in the West Bank and Gaza Strip, founded in 1987 to mount violent resistance to Israel and form an Islamic state. It won the Palestinian elections of 2006 and formed the government of the PA.

helicopter gunship military helicopter armed with machine guns, rockets and cannon for attacking targets on the ground

Hezbollah fighting organization and political party formed in 1982 to resist the Israeli invasion of Lebanon and form an Islamic state. It carried out a guerrilla campaign against Israel until Israel withdrew in 2000, and fought it during the Israel–Lebanon war in 2006.

Histadrut Israeli workers' organization that includes workers in most industries and also markets goods, builds settlements, runs banks and major companies and is responsible for a health service and educational activities

IDF (Israel Defence Forces) Israel's military, combining land, air and sea forces. All Jewish people in Israel have to perform military service.

intifada uprising of Palestinians against the Israeli military occupation of the West Bank and Gaza Strip

Islamic Jihad militant Palestinian Islamic movement that aims to destroy Israel and replace it with an Islamic Palestinian state. It has carried out many suicide bombings against Israel.

Knesset the Israeli Parliament

Labour Party on the left of Israeli politics, it has usually supported the idea of returning land to the Palestinians in return for peace

Likud Party on the right of Israeli politics, it has generally disagreed with giving back land to the Palestinians or dismantling Jewish settlements. Many members disagreed with the disengagement from Gaza in 2005 and the party split.

Mossad Israel's leading intelligence agency, which carries out undercover operations against Israel's enemies

PA (Palestinian Authority) governing body of the Palestinians responsible for civil services in the Palestinian-ruled areas of the West Bank and Gaza Strip since 1994

PLO (Palestinian Liberation Organization) a political organization set up in 1964 that claims to represent the world's Palestinians.

PFLP (Popular Front for the Liberation of Palestine) left-wing organization within the PLO established in 1967. It rejected political compromise with Israel and organized many terrorist attacks against Israeli and Western interests.

suicide bombing attack by an individual using explosives in which the bomber is killed along with his or her victims

United Nations international organization formed in 1945 to try to maintain peace between countries.

White Paper

Yishuv Jewish community in Palestine from the 19th century until the formation of the State of Israel in 1948

Zionist before 1948, a person who supported the establishment of a state for the Jewish people in Palestine; after 1948, a person who supports Israel

Further Information

BOOKS

FOR CHILDREN

Simon Adams, *Israel and Palestine* (Franklin Watts, 2004)

David Downing, *Arafat* (Heinemann Library, 2003)

John King, *Israel and Palestine* (Raintree, 2005)

Phillip Marguiles, *Hamas: Palestinian Terrorists* (Rosen Publishing Group, 2004)

Stewart Ross, *Arab–Israeli Conflict* (Evans Brothers, 2004)

Cath Senker, *The Arab–Israeli Conflict* (Hodder Wayland, 2004)

Alex Woolf, *The Arab–Israeli Conflict* (World Almanac Education, 2004)

FOR OLDER READERS

Ahron Bregman, *Elusive Peace: How the Holy Land Defeated America* (Penguin Books, 2005)

Ahron Bregman and Jihan el-Tahri, *The Fifty Years War: Israel and the Arabs* (Penguin, 1998)

Martin Gilbert, *Israel: A History* (Doubleday, 1998)

Benny Morris, *Righteous Victims: A History of the Zionist–Arab Conflict 1881–2001* (Vintage Books, 2001)

DVD

The Shape of the Future – a documentary looking at the history of the conflict and the possibilities for peace (2004)

WEBSITES

http://news.bbc.co.uk/cbbcnews/hi/findout/guides/world/middle_east newsid_1602700/1602748.stm
– BBC *Newsround's* guide to the Middle East conflict

http://www.btselem.org/English/
– the site for B'tselem, an Israeli human rights organization

http://www.israel-mfa.gov.il/MFA
– the official Israeli government website, with facts about Israel, its history and the peace process

http://www.mideastweb.org/
– MidEastWeb is a non-governmental organization in Israel that aims to promote dialogue between Arabs, Jews and others

Index

Numbers in **bold** refer to photographs or, where indicated, to maps.